Hummingbirds

Written by Jenny Feely

Flying Start
to Literacy®

Contents

Introduction

Hummingbirds are the smallest birds in the world. Like most birds, they can fly, but they are the only birds that can fly in any direction. As well as flying forwards, they can fly backwards and even upside down.

Also, hummingbirds are the only birds that can stay in the one place in the air. This is called hovering.

Hovering is very important for hummingbirds because it is how they get food to stay alive.

Chapter 1: Body basics

Hummingbirds have small, light bodies and strong, fast-moving wings to help them fly. They have long, thin bills and long tongues to help them get food.

Fact box

A hummingbird is about 8 centimetres from the tip of its bill to the tip of its tail. It weighs between 2 and 20 grams.

Hummingbird feathers have no colour.
They are filled with small sacs of air that
reflect the light in bright flashes.

Hummingbirds have large brains for their
size and fast-beating hearts.

Flying

Hummingbirds have small, weak feet and legs, and cannot walk. They can only move around by flying.

When hummingbirds fly, their wings move so quickly that they are a blur. This makes a humming sound and is how these birds got their name.

When they are not flying, hummingbirds rest on branches.

Fact box

When they are flying, hummingbirds flap
their wings more than 80 times per second.

Chapter 2: Food

Hummingbirds eat nectar from flowers. Nectar is a good food for hummingbirds because it gives them lots of energy.

When a hummingbird finds a flower, it hovers in the air. It puts its long, thin bill into the flower and sips the nectar with its long tongue.

Hummingbirds also eat small insects. They catch these insects by chasing them through the air and grabbing them with their bill.

It is important for hummingbirds to eat insects because it helps them to build muscles and stay strong.

Territory

A hummingbird uses lots of energy to fly, so it has to make sure that it always has flowers to feed from. It does this by taking an area that has all the food, water and nectar that it needs. This area is the hummingbird's territory.

Fact box

Hummingbirds have to find flowers to feed from every 15 minutes.

A hummingbird will stop other hummingbirds from coming into its territory. It does this by flashing its bright feathers, which scares away other birds.

This hummingbird is warning another hummingbird to stay away from its territory.

13

A hummingbird never forgets

Hummingbirds have excellent memories. This helps them to find food without wasting energy. They can remember which flowers they have already visited, even when there are a lot of flowers on one plant. They can also remember when certain flowers will be in bloom. This helps them to save energy.

At night, a hummingbird sleeps and cannot feed. When it sleeps, it slows down its heartbeat so that it does not use much energy.

In the morning, the hummingbird wakes up by shivering hard. This makes its heart beat faster.

Chapter 3:
Chicks and eggs

When a hummingbird is ready to mate, the male hummingbird shows off its bright colours and does flying tricks to attract a female.

The female hummingbird builds a nest and looks after the eggs and the chicks by herself.

When the chicks hatch, their mother leaves the nest to find nectar. When the mother returns to the nest, she feeds the nectar to the chicks.

While the chicks wait for their mother to return, they stay very still and make no noise. This helps them to keep safe from animals that might eat them.

Hummingbird chicks grow quickly. When they are about three weeks old, they leave the nest and start to find their own food.

Chapter 4:
An amazing flight

Ruby-throated hummingbirds live in parts of North America. Each year just before winter, all the flowers where they live die, so there is no food for them to eat. These hummingbirds fly south to Mexico where there are lots of flowers.

Just before winter, ruby-throated hummingbirds fly from North America to Mexico. This journey is often more than 800 kilometres long.

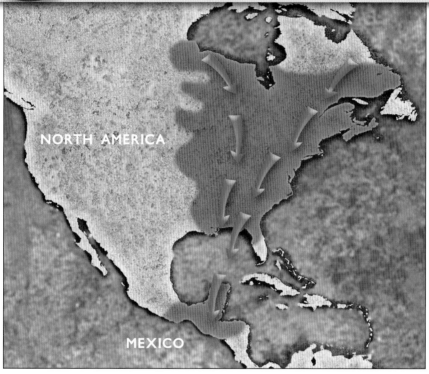

NORTH AMERICA

MEXICO

Some of these hummingbirds have to fly over the sea to reach Mexico. When they reach the coast, the hummingbirds stop for three or four days to eat and eat and eat. They store body fat, which gives them the energy they need for the long flight over the sea.

People put out bird feeders to help the hummingbirds on this long and difficult journey.

In spring, the hummingbirds fly back to North America to feed on the flowers that grow there.

This hummingbird is feeding from a bird feeder.

Conclusion

Hummingbirds may be the smallest of all the birds, but their small size doesn't stop them from doing amazing things. They can do things that bigger, heavier birds cannot do. And some of these things are remarkable.